www.providencebooks.net

Publisher Contact

Email:contact@providencebooks.net

Social media: facebook.com/providencebooks

Acknowledgements

The team at Providence Books would like to thank our friends, family, suppliers and customers for making our vision of creating the highest-quality books a reality. Thanks for purchasing and enjoy the quotes!

This page is intentionally left blank

This page is intentionally left blank

3D is a way of organizing things, particularly as we're getting much more media information on the computer, a lot more choices, a lot more navigation than we've ever had before.

Bill Gates

640K ought to be enough for anybody.

Bill Gates

A first-generation fortune is the most likely to be given away, but once a fortune is inherited it's less likely that a very high percentage will go back to society.

Bill Gates

A lot of people assume that creating software is purely a solitary activity where you sit in an office with the door closed all day and write lots of code.

Bill Gates

A lot of the things that will really improve the world fortunately aren't dependent on Washington doing something different.

Bill Gates

AIDS itself is subject to incredible stigma.

Bill Gates

According to Ethiopian custom, parents wait to name a baby because children often die in the first weeks of life.

Bill Gates

Africa is on the rise.

Bill Gates

Almost every way we make electricity today, except for the emerging renewables and nuclear, puts out CO2. And so, what we're going to have to do at a global scale, is create a new system. And so, we need energy miracles.

Bill Gates

Although I don't have a prescription for what others should do, I know I have been very fortunate and feel a responsibility to give back to society in a very significant way.

Bill Gates

Americans move more than 10 times over the course of a lifetime.

Bill Gates

Americans want students to get the best education possible. We want schools to prepare children to become good citizens and members of a prosperous American economy.

Bill Gates

Antitrust is the way that the government promotes markets when there are market failures. It has nothing to do with the idea of free information.

Bill Gates

Any version of Windows is going to have lots of great new things that people use and things that are tough.

Bill Gates

Apple has always leveraged technologies that the PC industry has driven to critical mass - the bus structures, the graphics cards, the peripherals, the connection networks, things like that - so they're kind of in the PC ecosystem and kind of not.

Bill Gates

As we look ahead into the next century, leaders will be those who empower others.

Bill Gates

At Microsoft there are lots of brilliant ideas but the image is that they all come from the top - I'm afraid that's not quite right.

Bill Gates

Being able to see an activity log of where a kid has been going on the Internet is a good thing.

Bill Gates

Being flooded with information doesn't mean we have the right information or that we're in touch with the right people.

Bill Gates

Bitcoin is mostly about anonymous transactions, and I don't think over time that's a good way to go. I'm a huge believe in digital currency... but doing it on an anonymous basis I think that leads to some abuses, so I'm not involved in Bitcoin.

Bill Gates

By 2018, an estimated 63 percent of all new U.S. jobs will require workers with an education beyond high school. For our young people to get those jobs, they first need to graduate from high school ready to start a postsecondary education.

Bill Gates

By 2035, there will be almost no poor countries left in the world. Almost all countries will be what we now call lower-middle income or richer.

Bill Gates

By improving health, empowering women, population growth comes down.

Bill Gates

By the time we see that climate change is really bad, your ability to fix it is extremely limited... The carbon gets up there, but the heating effect is delayed. And then the effect of that heat on the species and ecosystem is delayed. That means that even when you turn virtuous, things are actually going to get worse for quite a while.

Bill Gates

Capitalism has shortfalls. It doesn't necessarily take care of the poor, and it underfunds innovation, so we have to offset that.

Bill Gates

Capitalism has worked very well. Anyone who wants to move to North Korea is welcome.

Bill Gates

Certainly I'll never be able to put myself in the situation that people growing up in the less developed countries are in. I've gotten a bit of a sense of it by being out there and meeting people and talking with them.

Bill Gates

Certainly there's a phenomenon around open source. You know free software will be a vibrant area. There will be a lot of neat things that get done there.

Bill Gates

Certainly, the Windows share of servers is strong.

Bill Gates

China adopted a capitalist system in the 1980s, and they went from a 60% poverty rate to 10%.

Bill Gates

China and the U.S. need each other very badly. Yes, we should argue about some things, but it's not an 'us versus them,' it's an 'us and them' type scenario.

Bill Gates

China has many successful entrepreneurs and business people. I hope that more people of insight will put their talents to work to improve the lives of poor people in China and around the world, and seek solutions for them.

Bill Gates

China is certainly an important player in the global economy, and a widespread AIDS epidemic would threaten that growth.

Bill Gates

Climate change is a terrible problem, and it absolutely needs to be solved. It deserves to be a huge priority.

Bill Gates

Common Core is a big win for education.

Bill Gates

Connectivity enables transparency for better government, education, and health.

Bill Gates

Considering their impact, you might expect mosquitoes to get more attention than they do. Sharks kill fewer than a dozen people every year, and in the U.S. they get a week dedicated to them on TV every year.

Bill Gates

Contrary to popular belief, I don't spend a whole lot of time following soccer. But as I have traveled around the world to better understand global development and health, I've learned that soccer is truly universal. No matter where I go, that's what kids are playing. That's what people are talking about.

Bill Gates

Corruption is one of the most common reasons I hear in views that criticize aid.

Bill Gates

Countries which receive aid do graduate. Within a generation, Korea went from being a big recipient to being a big aid donor. China used to get quite a bit of aid; now it's aid-neutral.

Bill Gates

DOS is ugly and interferes with users' experience.

Bill Gates

Digital reading will completely take over. It's lightweight and it's fantastic for sharing. Over time it will take over.

Bill Gates

Digital technology has several features that can make it much easier for teachers to pay special attention to all their students.

Bill Gates

Discrimination has a lot of layers that make it tough for minorities to get a leg up.

Bill Gates

Driving up the value of the advertising is a big commitment for Microsoft.

Bill Gates

Drones overall will be more impactful than I think people recognize, in positive ways to help society.

Bill Gates

Effective philanthropy requires a lot of time and creativity - the same kind of focus and skills that building a business requires.

Bill Gates

Employers have decided that having the breadth of knowledge that's associated with a four-year degree is often something they want to see in the people they give that job to.

Bill Gates

Energy innovation is not a nationalistic game.

Bill Gates

Eradications are special. Zero is a magic number. You either do what it takes to get to zero and you're glad you did it; or you get close, give up and it goes back to where it was before, in which case you wasted all that credibility, activity, money that could have been applied to other things.

Bill Gates

Even with cameras being very cheap, one thing that researchers noticed was that you look really bad in a videoconference image because the lighting is bad and you get shadows and things.

Bill Gates

Eventually we'll be able to sequence the human genome and replicate how nature did intelligence in a carbon-based system.

Bill Gates

Eventually you won't think of 'the Internet business.' You'll think of it more like news, weather, sports, but even that taxonomy isn't clear.

Bill Gates

Eventually, all companies are replaced.

Bill Gates

Everyone needs a coach. It doesn't matter whether you're a basketball player, a tennis player, a gymnast or a bridge player.

Bill Gates

Expectations are a form of first-class truth: If people believe it, it's true.

Bill Gates

Exposure from a young age to the realities of the world is a super-big thing.

Bill Gates

Flying cars are not a very efficient way to move things from one point to another.

Bill Gates

For Africa to move forward, you've really got to get rid of malaria.

Bill Gates

For a highly motivated learner, it's not like knowledge is secret and somehow the Internet made it not secret. It just made knowledge easy to find. If you're a motivated enough learner, books are pretty good.

Bill Gates

Fortunately for India, it has got a growing economy. If it is doing the right things with taxation and focusing on the right areas for human development, it is going to have no problem, over a period of time, taking care of its own needs.

Bill Gates

Given how few young people actually read the newspaper, it's a good thing they'll be reading a newspaper on a screen.

Bill Gates

Globalization has made copper and other minerals more valuable, and Ghana and Kenya have recently discovered mineral resources.

Bill Gates

Google's done a super good job on search; Apple's done a great job on the IPod.

Bill Gates

Governments will always play a huge part in solving big problems. They set public policy and are uniquely able to provide the resources to make sure solutions reach everyone who needs them. They also fund basic research, which is a crucial component of the innovation that improves life for everyone.

Bill Gates

Haiti should remind us all that there is an immediate need to invest in and promote long-term development projects that are sustainable, scalable, and proven to work.

Bill Gates

Harnessing steam power required many innovations, as William Rosen chronicles in the book 'The Most Powerful Idea in the World.'

Bill Gates

Headlines, in a way, are what mislead you because bad news is a headline, and gradual improvement is not.

Bill Gates

Helping convene global stakeholders to establish a set of measurable, actionable and consensus-built goals focused on extreme poverty is invaluable.

Bill Gates

Historically, privacy was almost implicit, because it was hard to find and gather information. But in the digital world, whether it's digital cameras or satellites or just what you click on, we need to have more explicit rules - not just for governments but for private companies.

Bill Gates

I actually thought that it would be a little confusing during the same period of your life to be in one meeting when you're trying to make money, and then go to another meeting where you're giving it away. I mean is it gonna erode your ability, you know, to make money? Are you gonna somehow get confused about what you're trying to do?

Bill Gates

I agree with people like Richard Dawkins that mankind felt the need for creation myths. Before we really began to understand disease and the weather and things like that, we sought false explanations for them. Now science has filled in some of the realm - not all - that religion used to fill.

Bill Gates

I believe in innovation and that the way you get innovation is you fund research and you learn the basic facts.

Bill Gates

I believe that if you show people the problems and you show them the solutions they will be moved to act.

Bill Gates

I believe the returns on investment in the poor are just as exciting as successes achieved in the business arena, and they are even more meaningful!

Bill Gates

I can understand wanting to have millions of dollars; there's a certain freedom, meaningful freedom, that comes with that.

Bill Gates

I didn't used to wear a watch. Now I have a SPOT watch, which I wear all the time.

Bill Gates

I don't generally read a lot of fiction.

Bill Gates

I don't have a magic formula for prioritizing the world's problems.

Bill Gates

I don't like typing messages on my phone. Some people get used to it.

Bill Gates

I don't think culture is something you can describe.

Bill Gates

I don't think there is any philosophy that suggests having polio is a good thing.

Bill Gates

I don't think there's a... boundary between digital media and print media. Every magazine is doing an online version.

Bill Gates

I don't think there's anything unique about human intelligence.

Bill Gates

I get more spam than anyone I know.

Bill Gates

I have a company that is not Microsoft, called Corbis. Corbis is the operation that merged with Bettman Archives. It has nothing to do with Microsoft. It was intentionally done outside of Microsoft because Microsoft isn't interested.

Bill Gates

I have a nice office. I have a nice house... So I'm not denying myself some great things. I just don't happen to have expensive hobbies.

Bill Gates

I have a particular relationship with Vinod Khosla because he's got a lot of very interesting science-based energy startups.

Bill Gates

I have an excellent memory, a most excellent memory.

Bill Gates

I have been struck again and again by how important measurement is to improving the human condition.

Bill Gates

I have seen firsthand that agricultural science has enormous potential to increase the yields of small farmers and lift them out of hunger and poverty.

Bill Gates

I know there's a farmer out there somewhere who never wants a PC and that's fine with me.

Bill Gates

I like the idea of putting your Christmas wish list up and letting people share it.

Bill Gates

I meet people overseas that know five languages - that the only language I'm comfortable in is English.

Bill Gates

I never took a day off in my twenties. Not one. And I'm still fanatical, but now I'm a little less fanatical.

Bill Gates

I read a lot of obscure books and it is nice to open a book.

Bill Gates

I really had a lot of dreams when I was a kid, and I think a great deal of that grew out of the fact that I had a chance to read a lot.

Bill Gates

I remember thinking quite logically that I didn't want to spoil my children with wealth and so that I would create a foundation, but not knowing exactly what it would focus on.

Bill Gates

I spend a lot of time reading.

Bill Gates

I think any statement about stock prices is always suspect unless it's made by Warren Buffett.

Bill Gates

I think it makes sense to believe in God, but exactly what decision in your life you make differently because of it, I don't know.

Bill Gates

I think it's fair to say that personal computers have become the most empowering tool we've ever created. They're tools of communication, they're tools of creativity, and they can be shaped by their user.

Bill Gates

I think that society has to be careful not to shift all of its resources to the elderly versus the young.

Bill Gates

I think the positive competition between states in India is one of the most positive dynamics that the country has.

Bill Gates

I think the thing we see is that as people are using video games more, they tend to watch passive TV a bit less. And so using the PC for the Internet, playing video games, is starting to cut into the rather unbelievable amount of time people spend watching TV.

Bill Gates

I think there will be PCs at every price point.

Bill Gates

I think when smallpox was eliminated, the whole world got pretty excited about that because it's just such a dramatic success.

Bill Gates

I understand how every healthy child, every new road, puts a country on a better path, but instability and war will arise from time to time, and I'm not an expert on how you get out of those things.

Bill Gates

I was a kind of hyper-intense person in my twenties and very impatient.

Bill Gates

I was lucky to be involved and get to contribute to something that was important, which is empowering people with software.

Bill Gates

I went to a public school through sixth grade, and being good at tests wasn't cool.

Bill Gates

I would counsel people to go to college, because it's one of the best times in your life in terms of who you meet and develop a broad set of intellectual skills.

Bill Gates

I'm a geek.

Bill Gates

I'm a great believer that any tool that enhances communication has profound effects in terms of how people can learn from each other, and how they can achieve the kind of freedoms that they're interested in.

Bill Gates

I'm an investor in a number of biotech companies, partly because of my incredible enthusiasm for the great innovations they will bring.

Bill Gates

I'm certainly well taken care of in terms of food and clothes.

Bill Gates

I'm going to retain a lot of Microsoft's stock.

Bill Gates

I'm going to save my public voice largely for the issues where I have some depth.

Bill Gates

I'm never fully satisfied with any Microsoft product.

Bill Gates

I'm not big on to-do lists. Instead, I use e-mail and desktop folders and my online calendar. So when I walk up to my desk, I can focus on the e-mails I've flagged and check the folders that are monitoring particular projects and particular blogs.

Bill Gates

I'm sorry that we have to have a Washington presence. We thrived during our first 16 years without any of this. I never made a political visit to Washington and we had no people here. It wasn't on our radar screen. We were just making great software.

Bill Gates

I've always been amazed by Da Vinci, because he worked out science on his own. He would work by drawing things and writing down his ideas. Of course, he designed all sorts of flying machines way before you could actually build something like that.

Bill Gates

I've always been interested in science - one of my favourite books is James Watson's 'Molecular Biology of the Gene.'

Bill Gates

I've been very lucky, and therefore I owe it to try and reduce the inequity in the world. And that's kind of a religious belief. I mean, it's at least a moral belief.

Bill Gates

If African farmers can use improved seeds and better practices to grow more crops and get them to market, then millions of families can earn themselves a better living and a better life.

Bill Gates

If GM had kept up with technology like the computer industry has, we would all be driving $25 cars that got 1,000 MPG.

Bill Gates

If I hadn't given my money away, I'd have had more than anyone else on the planet.

Bill Gates

If I'd had some set idea of a finish line, don't you think I would have crossed it years ago?

Bill Gates

If all my bridge coach ever told me was that I was 'satisfactory,' I would have no hope of ever getting better. How

would I know who was the best? How would I know what I
was doing differently?

Bill Gates

If people want capital gains taxed more like the highest rate on
income, that's a good discussion. Maybe that's the way to help
close the deficit.

Bill Gates

If you can't make it good, at least make it look good.

Bill Gates

If you count E-mail, I'm on the Internet all day, every day.

Bill Gates

If you go back to 1800, everybody was poor. I mean
everybody. The Industrial Revolution kicked in, and a lot of
countries benefited, but by no means everyone.

Bill Gates

If you have 50 different plug types, appliances wouldn't be
available and would be very expensive. But once an electric
outlet becomes standardized, many companies can design

appliances, and competition ensues, creating variety and better prices for consumers.

Bill Gates

If you're a person struggling to eat and stay healthy, you might have heard about Michael Jordan or Muhammad Ali, but you'll never have heard of Bill Gates.

Bill Gates

If you're low-income in the United States, you have a higher chance of going to jail than you do of getting a four-year degree. And that doesn't seem entirely fair.

Bill Gates

If you're using first-class land for biofuels, then you're competing with the growing of food. And so you're actually spiking food prices by moving energy production into agriculture.

Bill Gates

If you've found some way to educate yourself about engineering, stocks, or whatever it is, good employers will have some type of exam or interview and see a sample of your work.

Bill Gates

If your culture doesn't like geeks, you are in real trouble.

Bill Gates

In 80% of the world, energy will be bought where it is economic. You have to help the rest of the world get energy at a reasonable price.

Bill Gates

In American math classes, we teach a lot of concepts poorly over many years. In the Asian systems they teach you very few concepts very well over a few years.

Bill Gates

In K-12, almost everybody goes to local schools. Universities are a bit different because kids actually do pick the university. The bizarre thing, though, is that the merit of university is actually how good the students going in are: the SAT scores of the kids going in.

Bill Gates

In a budget, how important is art versus music versus athletics versus computer programming? At the end of the day, some of those trade-offs will be made politically.

Bill Gates

In almost every area of human endeavor, the practice improves over time. That hasn't been the case for teaching.

Bill Gates

In almost every job now, people use software and work with information to enable their organisation to operate more effectively.

Bill Gates

In business, the idea of measuring what you are doing, picking the measurements that count like customer satisfaction and performance... you thrive on that.

Bill Gates

In energy, you have to plan and do research way in advance, sometimes decades in advance to get a new system that's safer, doesn't require us to go around the world to get all our oil.

Bill Gates

In inner-city, low-income communities of color, there's such a high correlation in terms of educational quality and success.

Bill Gates

In low-income countries, getting to a health post is hard. It's very expensive.

Bill Gates

In low-income countries, the main problems you have is infectious diseases.

Bill Gates

In ninth grade, I came up with a new form of rebellion. I hadn't been getting good grades, but I decided to get all A's without taking a book home. I didn't go to math class, because I knew enough and had read ahead, and I placed within the top 10 people in the nation on an aptitude exam.

Bill Gates

In order for the United States to do the right things for the long term, it appears to be helpful for us to have the prospect of humiliation. Sputnik helped us fund good science - really good science: the semiconductor came out of it.

Bill Gates

In order to deal with all the medical cost demands and other challenges in the U.S., as we look to raise that revenue, the rich will have to pay slightly more. That's quite clear.

Bill Gates

In poor countries, we still need better ways to measure the effectiveness of the many government workers providing health services. They are the crucial link bringing tools such as vaccines and education to the people who need them most. How well trained are they? Are they showing up to work?

Bill Gates

In terms of mathematics textbooks, why can't you have the scale of a national market? Right now, we have a Texas textbook that's different from a California textbook that's different from a Massachusetts textbook. That's very expensive.

Bill Gates

In the long run, your human capital is your main base of competition. Your leading indicator of where you're going to be 20 years from now is how well you're doing in your education system.

Bill Gates

In the old generation, if one kid bought a PlayStation 2 and the other kid bought an Xbox, at his house you played PlayStation, at your house you played Xbox. Now that it's online, all those early buyers who... you want to play with, they've got their reputation online of who they are and how good they are at these games.

Bill Gates

In this business, by the time you realize you're in trouble, it's too late to save yourself. Unless you're running scared all the time, you're gone.

Bill Gates

India has over 20 percent of the kids born in the world. And they move around a lot.

Bill Gates

India is more of an aid recipient than a provider of aid.

Bill Gates

Information technology and business are becoming inextricably interwoven. I don't think anybody can talk meaningfully about one without the talking about the other.

Bill Gates

Innovation is a good thing. The human condition - put aside bioterrorism and a few footnotes - is improving because of innovation.

Bill Gates

Innovation is moving at a scarily fast pace.

Bill Gates

Innovations that are guided by smallholder farmers, adapted to local circumstances, and sustainable for the economy and environment will be necessary to ensure food security in the future.

Bill Gates

Intellectual property has the shelf life of a banana.

Bill Gates

Internet TV and the move to the digital approach is quite revolutionary. TV has historically has been a broadcast medium with everybody picking from a very finite number of channels.

Bill Gates

Investing for the poor requires participation from the entire community.

Bill Gates

It is hard to overstate how valuable it is to have all the incredible tools that are used for human disease to study plants.

Bill Gates

It's OK for China to invent cancer drugs that cure patients in the United States. We want them to catch up. But as the leader, we want to keep setting a very, very high standard. We don't want them to catch up because we're slowing down or, even worse, going into reverse.

Bill Gates

It's a nice reader, but there's nothing on the iPad I look at and say, 'Oh, I wish Microsoft had done it.'

Bill Gates

It's easier to add things on to a PC than it's ever been before. It's one click, and boom, it comes down.

Bill Gates

It's fine to celebrate success but it is more important to heed the lessons of failure.

Bill Gates

It's hard to improve public education - that's clear.

Bill Gates

It's possible - you can never know - that the universe exists only for me. If so, it's sure going well for me, I must admit.

Bill Gates

It's the poorer people in tropical zones who will get really hit by climate change - as well as some ecosystems, which nobody wants to see disappear.

Bill Gates

Just in terms of allocation of time resources, religion is not very efficient. There's a lot more I could be doing on a Sunday morning.

Bill Gates

K to 12 is partly about babysitting the kids so the parents can do other things.

Bill Gates

Lectures should go from being like the family singing around the piano to high-quality concerts.

Bill Gates

Legacy is a stupid thing! I don't want a legacy.

Bill Gates

Like almost everyone who uses e-mail, I receive a ton of spam every day. Much of it offers to help me get out of debt or get rich quick. It would be funny if it weren't so exciting.

Bill Gates

Like any well designed software product, Windows is designed, developed and tested as an integrated whole.

Bill Gates

Like my friend Warren Buffett, I feel particularly lucky to do something every day that I love to do. He calls it 'tap-dancing to work.'

Bill Gates

Living on $6 a day means you have a refrigerator, a TV, a cell phone, your children can go to school. That's not possible on $1 a day.

Bill Gates

Maintaining a consistent platform also helps improve product support - a significant problem in the software industry.

Bill Gates

Me and my dad are the biggest promoters of an estate tax in the US. It's not a popular position.

Bill Gates

Measles will always show you if someone isn't doing a good job on vaccinations. Kids will start dying of measles.

Bill Gates

Microsoft Research has a thing called the Sense Cam that, as you walk around, it's taking photos all the time. And the software will filter and find the ones that are interesting without having to think, 'Let's get out the camera and get that shot.' You just have that, and software helps you pick what you want.

Bill Gates

Microsoft is not about greed. It's about innovation and fairness.

Bill Gates

Middle-income countries are the biggest users of GMOs. Places like Brazil.

Bill Gates

Money has always been in politics. And I'm not sure you'd want money to be completely out of politics.

Bill Gates

Money has no utility to me beyond a certain point.

Bill Gates

Most poor people live in the poorest countries.

Bill Gates

Music, even with these dial-up connections you have to the Internet, is very practical to download.

Bill Gates

My experience of malaria was just taking anti-malarials, which give you strange dreams, because I don't want to get malaria.

Bill Gates

My mom and my dad were both very sociable, meeting lots of interesting people.

Bill Gates

My mom was on the United Way group that decides how to allocate the money and looks at all the different charities and makes the very hard decisions about where that pool of funds is going to go.

Bill Gates

My son likes to go see mines and electric plants, or the Large Hadron Collider, and we've had a chance to see a lot of interesting stuff.

Bill Gates

My wife thinks she's better than me at puzzles. I haven't given in on that one yet.

Bill Gates

Netscape was able to get the government working on its behalf.

Bill Gates

Newspaper readership is still growing in India.

Bill Gates

Nigeria has moved into low-middle-income, but their north is very poor, and the health care systems there have broken down.

Bill Gates

Ninety percent of the cases of polio are in security-vulnerable areas.

Bill Gates

No one person controls Microsoft. The board and the shareholders decide whether they want to have me as CEO.

Bill Gates

Nobody believes in completely unadulterated capitalism.

Bill Gates

Nobody spends any money on smallpox unless they worry about a bio-terrorist recreating it.

Bill Gates

Now everyone takes it for granted that you can look up movie reviews, track locations, and order stuff online. I wish there was a way we could take it away from people for a day so they could remember what it was like without it.

Bill Gates

Now, we put out a lot of carbon dioxide every year, over 26 billion tons. For each American, it's about 20 tons. For people in poor countries, it's less than one ton. It's an average of about five tons for everyone on the planet. And, somehow, we have to make changes that will bring that down to zero.

Bill Gates

Nuclear energy, in terms of an overall safety record, is better than other energy.

Bill Gates

OK, I have a nickname. My family calls me 'Trey' because I'm William the third. My dad has the same name, which is always confusing because my dad is well known, and I'm also known.

Bill Gates

Of my mental cycles, I devote maybe ten percent to business thinking. Business isn't that complicated. I wouldn't want to put it on my business card.

Bill Gates

Oh, I think there are a lot of people who would be buying and selling online today that go up there and they get the information, but then when it comes time to type in their credit card they think twice because they're not sure about how that might get out and what that might mean for them.

Bill Gates

On my desk I have three screens, synchronized to form a single desktop. I can drag items from one screen to the next. Once you have that large display area, you'll never go back, because it has a direct impact on productivity.

Bill Gates

One of the statistics that always amazes me is the approval of the Chinese government, not elected, is over 80 percent. The approval of the U.S. government, fully elected, is 19 percent. Well, we elected these people and they didn't elect those people. Isn't it supposed to be different? Aren't we supposed to like the people that we elected?

Bill Gates

One thing I've always loved about the culture at Microsoft is there is nobody who is tougher on us, in terms of what we need to learn and do better, than the people in the company itself.

You can walk down these halls, and they'll tell you, 'We need to do usability better, push this or that frontier.'

Bill Gates

Our teachers deserve better feedback.

Bill Gates

Outlook 2003 did create the idea of search folders and the whole Longhorn philosophy. You can see it at work in search folders, where instead of having to drop things into individual folders, and things exist only in one folder, you create these search folders and you have the criteria for the search folder.

Bill Gates

Over time, yes, countries will need to look at specific GMO products like they look at drugs today, where they don't approve them all. They look hard at the safety and the testing. And they make sure that the benefits far outweigh any of the downsides.

Bill Gates

Paper is no longer a big part of my day. I get 90% of my news online, and when I go to a meeting and want to jot things down, I bring my Tablet PC. It's fully synchronized with my office machine, so I have all the files I need. It also has a note-taking piece of software called OneNote, so all my notes are in digital form.

Bill Gates

People always fear change. People feared electricity when it was invented, didn't they? People feared coal, they feared gas-powered engines... There will always be ignorance, and ignorance leads to fear. But with time, people will come to accept their silicon masters.

Bill Gates

People are always coming up to me and saying, 'I heard your dad's speech, and it's really great.' And they'll mention some place I didn't even know my dad was going to.

Bill Gates

People are going to buy cheap fertilizer so they can grow enough crops to feed themselves, which will be increasingly difficult with climate change.

Bill Gates

People are using Windows PCs more than they watch TV now.

Bill Gates

People don't want lots and lots of single purpose devices. They do not want to have to learn how to set up something for photos, another thing for music, another thing for video.

Bill Gates

People everywhere love Windows.

Bill Gates

People should just buy a CD and rip it. You are legal then.

Bill Gates

People want to watch whatever video they want to watch whenever they want to watch. If you provision your Internet infrastructure adequately, you can do that.

Bill Gates

Personally, I'd like to see more of our leaders take a technocratic approach to solving our biggest problems.

Bill Gates

Philanthropy should be taking much bigger risks that business. If these are easy problems, business and government can come in and solve them.

Bill Gates

Philanthropy should be voluntary.

Bill Gates

Polio's pretty special because once you get an eradication, you no longer have to spend money on it; it's just there as a gift for the rest of time.

Bill Gates

Really advanced civilization is based on advances in energy.

Bill Gates

Research shows that there is only half as much variation in student achievement between schools as there is among classrooms in the same school. If you want your child to get the best education possible, it is actually more important to get him assigned to a great teacher than to a great school.

Bill Gates

Rich countries can afford to overpay for things.

Bill Gates

SPAM is taking e-mail, which is a wonderful tool, and exploiting the idea that it's very inexpensive to send mail.

Bill Gates

Security guys break the Mac every single day. Every single day, they come out with a total exploit; your machine can be taken over totally.

Bill Gates

Security is, I would say, our top priority because for all the exciting things you will be able to do with computers - organizing your lives, staying in touch with people, being creative - if we don't solve these security problems, then people will hold back.

Bill Gates

Should surveillance be usable for petty crimes like jaywalking or minor drug possession? Or is there a higher threshold for certain information? Those aren't easy questions.

Bill Gates

Should there be cameras everywhere in outdoor streets? My personal view is having cameras in inner cities is a very good thing. In the case of London, petty crime has gone down. They catch terrorists because of it. And if something really bad happens, most of the time you can figure out who did it.

Bill Gates

Since when has the world of computer software design been about what people want? This is a simple question of evolution. The day is quickly coming when every knee will bow down to a silicon fist, and you will all beg your binary gods for mercy.

Bill Gates

Skype actually does get a fair bit of revenue.

Bill Gates

Software innovation, like almost every other kind of innovation, requires the ability to collaborate and share ideas with other people, and to sit down and talk with customers and get their feedback and understand their needs.

Bill Gates

Software is a great combination between artistry and engineering.

Bill Gates

Software substitution, whether it's for drivers or waiters or nurses - it's progressing. Technology over time will reduce demand for jobs, particularly at the lower end of skill set.

Bill Gates

Some people, through luck and skill, end up with a lot of assets. If you're good at kicking a ball, writing software, investing in stocks, it pays extremely well.

Bill Gates

Some very poor countries run great vaccination systems, and some richer ones run terrible programs.

Bill Gates

Steve Jobs' ability to focus in on a few things that count, get people who get user interface right, and market things as revolutionary are amazing things.

Bill Gates

Success is a lousy teacher. It seduces smart people into thinking they can't lose.

Bill Gates

Teaching's hard! You need different skills: positive reinforcement, keeping students from getting bored, commanding their attention in a certain way.

Bill Gates

Technology is just a tool. In terms of getting the kids working together and motivating them, the teacher is the most important.

Bill Gates

Technology is unlocking the innate compassion we have for our fellow human beings.

Bill Gates

The 'Billionaire' song is what my kids tease me with. They sing it to me. It's funny.

Bill Gates

The AIDS is a disease that is hard to talk about.

Bill Gates

The Center for Disease Control started out as the malaria war control board based in Atlanta. Partly because the head of Coke had some people out to his plantation, and they got infected with malaria, and partly 'cause all the military recruits were coming down and having a higher fatality rate from malaria while training than in the field.

Bill Gates

The Gates Foundation has learned that two questions can predict how much kids learn: 'Does your teacher use class time well?' and, 'When you're confused, does your teacher help you get straightened out?'

Bill Gates

The Global Fund is a central player in the progress being achieved on HIV, TB and malaria. It channels resources to help countries fight these diseases. I believe in its impact because I have seen it firsthand.

Bill Gates

The Green Revolution focused on the big three - maize, rice and wheat - and the Green Revolution did not adapt the big three to African conditions, other than South Africa, as much as they should have.

Bill Gates

The Internet is becoming the town square for the global village of tomorrow.

Bill Gates

The Internet is the easiest thing to get into. To be an Internet retailer, you just get that URL.

Bill Gates

The PC has improved the world in just about every area you can think of. Amazing developments in communications, collaboration and efficiencies. New kinds of entertainment and social media. Access to information and the ability to give a voice people who would never have been heard.

Bill Gates

The U.S. couldn't even get rid of Saddam Hussein. And we all know that the EU is just a passing fad. They'll be killing each other again in less than a year. I'm sick to death of all these fascist lawsuits.

Bill Gates

The U.S. immigration laws are bad - really, really bad. I'd say treatment of immigrants is one of the greatest injustices done in our government's name.

Bill Gates

The ability of a successful company to add functionality to its product has long been upheld.

Bill Gates

The advance of technology is based on making it fit in so that you don't really even notice it, so it's part of everyday life.

Bill Gates

The belief that the world is getting worse, that we can't solve extreme poverty and disease, isn't just mistaken. It is harmful.

Bill Gates

The best teacher is very interactive.

Bill Gates

The bulk of the universities are about teaching kids.

Bill Gates

The common thread for everything I do is this idea of a Web-services architecture. What does that mean? It means taking components of software and systems and having them be self-describing, so that you can aim them, ask them what their capabilities are, and communicate with them using a standard protocol.

Bill Gates

The difference between a stranger sending you a message that you might be interested in at a very low volume level, no repetition, just sending it to very few people, and that being done as spam - those things get close enough that you want to be careful never to filter out something that's legitimate.

Bill Gates

The fight against AIDS in China is already well underway. The Chinese government and other funders are providing major support, and they'll continue to bear primary responsibility for delivering prevention and treatment.

Bill Gates

The first rule of any technology used in a business is that automation applied to an efficient operation will magnify the efficiency. The second is that automation applied to an inefficient operation will magnify the inefficiency.

Bill Gates

The future of Windows is to let the computer see, listen and even learn.

Bill Gates

The future of advertising is the Internet.

Bill Gates

The general idea of the rich helping the poor, I think, is important.

Bill Gates

The idea that you encourage companies to take their innovative thinkers and think about the most needy - even beyond the market opportunities - that's something that appropriately ought to be done.

Bill Gates

The ideal thing would be to have a 100 percent effective AIDS vaccine. And to have broad usage of that vaccine. That would literally break the epidemic.

Bill Gates

The intersection of law, politics, and technology is going to force a lot of good thinking.

Bill Gates

The kids are a big part of my schedule.

Bill Gates

The main thing that's missing in energy is an incentive to create things that are zero-CO2-emitting and that have the right scale and reliability characteristics.

Bill Gates

The mainstream is always under attack.

Bill Gates

The malaria parasite has been killing children and sapping the strength of whole populations for tens of thousands of years. It is impossible to calculate the harm malaria has done to the world.

Bill Gates

The microprocessor is a miracle.

Bill Gates

The misconception that aid falls straight into the hands of dictators largely stems from the Cold War era.

Bill Gates

The moral systems of religion, I think, are super important.

Bill Gates

The most amazing philanthropists are people who are actually making a significant sacrifice.

Bill Gates

The most impactful dollars that Australia can spend are actually what goes to help the poorest.

Bill Gates

The most interesting biofuel efforts avoid using land that's expensive and has high opportunity costs. They do this by getting onto other types of land, or taking advantage of byproducts that aren't used in the food chain today, or by intercropping.

Bill Gates

The next time someone tells you we can trim the budget by cutting aid, I hope you will ask whether it will come at the cost of more people dying.

Bill Gates

The nuclear approach I'm involved in is called a traveling-wave reactor, which uses waste uranium for fuel. There's a lot of things that have to go right for that dream to come true - many decades of building demo plants, proving the economics are right. But if it does, you could have cheaper energy with no CO_2 emissions.

Bill Gates

The nuclear industry has this amazing record, even equipment from generations one and two. But nuclear mishaps tend to come in these big events - Chernobyl, Three Mile Island, and now Fukushima - so it's more visible.

Bill Gates

The only definition by which America's best days are behind it is on a purely relative basis.

Bill Gates

The only thing I understand deeply, because in my teens I was thinking about it, and every year of my life, is software. So I'll never be hands-on on anything except software.

Bill Gates

The outpouring of support from millions of people in the immediate aftermath of the earthquake in Haiti has been impressive.

Bill Gates

The outside perception and inside perception of Microsoft are so different. The view of Microsoft inside Microsoft is always kind of an underdog thing.

Bill Gates

The part of uranium that's fissile - when you hit it with a neutron, it splits in two - is about 0.7%. The reactors we have today are burning that 0.7%.

Bill Gates

The potential financial reward for building the 'next Windows' is so great that there will never be a shortage of new technologies seeking to challenge it.

Bill Gates

The protestor I think will speak up for the world's poorest.

Bill Gates

The quality of research in the U.S. is absolutely the best.

Bill Gates

The spread of online information isn't just good for charities. It's also good for donors. You can go to a site like Charity Navigator, which evaluates nonprofits on their financial health as well as the amount of information they share about their work.

Bill Gates

The tablet is not mainstream. Reading off the screen is not mainstream.

Bill Gates

The thing about HD-DVD that is attractive to Microsoft is that it's very pro-consumer in letting you copy all movies up onto the hard disk.

Bill Gates

The tool that's most associated with the recent progress against malaria is the long-lasting bed net. Bed nets are a fantastic innovation. But we can do even better. We can invent new ways to control the mosquitoes that carry the malaria parasite.

Bill Gates

The trouble with energy farming is that the energy isn't always where you want to use it, and it isn't always when you want to use it.

Bill Gates

The truth of Moore's law has made remarkable things possible. On the software side, I think natural user interfaces in all their forms are equally significant.

Bill Gates

The typical project design time for a large company like IBM - and they keep track of this - is a little over four years.

Bill Gates

The way to be successful in the software world is to come up with breakthrough software, and so whether it's Microsoft Office or Windows, its pushing that forward. New ideas, surprising the marketplace, so good engineering and good business are one in the same.

Bill Gates

The world at large is less inequitable today than at any time in history. Number of people in abject poverty, as a percentage, is at all-time low.

Bill Gates

The world has been very careful to pick very few diseases for eradication, because it is very tough.

Bill Gates

The world is not flat, and PCs are not, in the hierarchy of human needs, in the first five rungs.

Bill Gates

The worst pandemic in modern history was the Spanish flu of 1918, which killed tens of millions of people. Today, with how interconnected the world is, it would spread faster.

Bill Gates

The year I was born, 1955, the first big disease-eradication program in the world was declared for malaria. After about a decade of work, they realized that, at least in the tropical areas, they did not have the tools to get it done.

Bill Gates

There are GMO skeptics more in Europe maybe than in other places, but not exclusively.

Bill Gates

There are more people dying of malaria than any specific cancer.

Bill Gates

There are people who don't like capitalism, and people who don't like PCs. But there's no-one who likes the PC who doesn't like Microsoft.

Bill Gates

There are websites that any government wants to block. The truth about the Internet is that it's extremely hard to block anything - extremely hard. You'll never get perfect blocking.

Bill Gates

There certainly is a case to be made that taxes should be more progressive.

Bill Gates

There is a difference between what technology enables and what historical business practices enable.

Bill Gates

There is no author whose books I look forward to more than Vaclav Smil.

Bill Gates

There is no doubt that as an economy grows in a great way like India has, that you have to step back and change your tax systems, because you start to get more disparities of wealth.

Bill Gates

There's 20 companies that I have investments in - some batteries, some solar-thermal, one big nuclear thing. We need hundreds and hundreds of companies like that, so that in a 20-year time frame we really are starting to change the energy infrastructure.

Bill Gates

There's always been a lot of information about your activities. Every phone number you dial, every credit-card charge you make. It's long since passed that a typical person doesn't leave footprints.

Bill Gates

There's no magic line between an application and an operating system that some bureaucrat in Washington should draw.

Bill Gates

There's no such thing as going to a soapbox and saying, 'The government's corrupt,' and not having the intelligence service see your face. In the digital world, that can be done.

Bill Gates

This is a fantastic time to be entering the business world, because business is going to change more in the next 10 years than it has in the last 50.

Bill Gates

This social-networking thing takes you to crazy places.

Bill Gates

This whole phenomenon of the computer in a library is an amazing thing.

Bill Gates

To create a new standard, it takes something that's not just a little bit different; it takes something that's really new and really captures people's imagination, and the Macintosh, of all the machines I've ever seen, is the only one that meets that standard.

Bill Gates

Today, we're very dependent on cheap energy. We just take it for granted - all the things you have in the house, the way industry works.

Bill Gates

Treatment without prevention is simply unsustainable.

Bill Gates

Two out of every five people on Earth today owe their lives to the higher crop outputs that fertilizer has made possible.

Bill Gates

Typically, your corporate e-mail account is not, today, that spam-targeted. It's more the free e-mail accounts that are spam-targeted.

Bill Gates

U.K. companies are in very international and very competitive markets. If you look at PC penetration in the U.K., it is very similar to the United States market.

Bill Gates

Understanding science and pushing the boundaries of science is what makes me immensely satisfied.

Bill Gates

Unemployment rates among Americans who never went to college are about double that of those who have a postsecondary education.

Bill Gates

Unfortunately, the highly curious student is a small percentage of the kids.

Bill Gates

Until we're educating every kid in a fantastic way, until every inner city is cleaned up, there is no shortage of things to do.

Bill Gates

We all know that there are these exemplars who can take the toughest students, and they'll teach them two-and-a-half years of math in a single year.

Bill Gates

We all need people who will give us feedback. That's how we improve.

Bill Gates

We all sort of do want incentives for creative people to still exist at a certain level. You know, maybe rock stars shouldn't make as much; who knows? But you want as much creativity to take place in the future as took place in the past.

Bill Gates

We always overestimate the change that will occur in the next two years and underestimate the change that will occur in the next ten. Don't let yourself be lulled into inaction.

Bill Gates

We are in the throes of a transition where every publication has to think of their digital strategy.

BIll Gates

We are not even close to finishing the basic dream of what the PC can be.

Bill Gates

We have to find a way to make the aspects of capitalism that serve wealthier people serve poorer people as well.

Bill Gates

We make the future sustainable when we invest in the poor, not when we insist on their suffering.

Bill Gates

We should all grow our own food and do our own waste processing, we really should.

Bill Gates

We've got to put a lot of money into changing behavior.

Bill Gates

Well I think any author or musician is anxious to have legitimate sales of their products, partly so they're rewarded for their success, partly so they can go on and do new things.

Bill Gates

Well private money can take risks in a way that government money often isn't willing to.

Bill Gates

Well the protester I think is a very powerful thing. It's basically a mechanism of democracy that, along with capitalism, scientific innovation, those things have built the modern world. And it's wonderful that the new tools have empowered that protestor so that state secrets, bad developments are not hidden anymore.

Bill Gates

Well, I don't think there's any need for people to focus on my career.

Bill Gates

Well, no one gives aid to Zimbabwe through the Mugabe government.

Bill Gates

Well-spent aid money is saving lives for a few thousand dollars per life saved.

Bill Gates

What destroys more self-confidence than any other educational thing in America is being assigned to some remedial math when you get into some college, and then it's not taught very well and you end up with this sense of, 'Hey, I can't really figure those things out.'

Bill Gates

What's amazing is, if young people understood how doing well in school makes the rest of their life so much interesting, they would be more motivated. It's so far away in time that they can't appreciate what it means for their whole life.

Bill Gates

When Ford sells a car, a dealer isn't allowed to take out the engine and put a different one in. When a newsstand sells the Washington Post, no one can go to the newsstand and pay them to rip out the classified section and put their own classified section in - if they could, they would do so.

Bill Gates

When I was growing up, my parents were almost involved in various volunteer things. My dad was head of Planned Parenthood. And it was very controversial to be involved with that.

Bill Gates

When I was in my 40s, Microsoft was my primary activity.

Bill Gates

When Paul Allen and I started Microsoft over 30 years ago, we had big dreams about software. We had dreams about the impact it could have.

Bill Gates

When a country has the skill and self-confidence to take action against its biggest problems, it makes outsiders eager to be a part of it.

Bill Gates

When the PC was launched, people knew it was important.

Bill Gates

When you revolutionize education, you're taking the very mechanism of how people be smarter and do new things, and you're priming the pump for so many incredible things.

Bill Gates

When you want to do your homework, fill out your tax return, or see all the choices for a trip you want to take, you need a full-size screen.

Bill Gates

Whenever you have multiple devices including multiple PCs that you want to share information with, it's always been a bit complicated.

Bill Gates

Whether I'm at the office, at home, or on the road, I always have a stack of books I'm looking forward to reading.

Bill Gates

Whether it's Google or Apple or free software, we've got some fantastic competitors and it keeps us on our toes.

Bill Gates

Who decides what's in Windows? The customers who buy it.

Bill Gates

Windows 8 is key to the future, the Surface computer.

Bill Gates

Windows is probably the most important product in the entire PC industry. Everything we do in terms of supporting touch, new hardware, accessibility has incredible impact.

Bill Gates

With Windows 8, Microsoft is trying to gain market share in what has been dominated by the iPad-type device. But a lot of those users are frustrated. They can't type. They can't create documents.

Bill Gates

With tech companies, whoever's the leader is always questioned, you know. They say, 'Is this the end of them?' And - there's more - more times people think that's the case than it really is the case.

Bill Gates

You can always think of something like the Xbox 360 as a super set-top box that can do everything the set-top box does, but then have the graphics to do the games as well.

Bill Gates

You can't have a rigid view that all new taxes are evil.

Bill Gates

You have to have a certain realism that government is a pretty blunt instrument, and without the constant attention of highly qualified people with the right metrics, it will fall into not doing things very well.

Bill Gates

You know capitalism is this wonderful thing that motivates people, it causes wonderful inventions to be done. But in this area of diseases of the world at large, it's really let us down.

Bill Gates

You may have heard of Black Friday and Cyber Monday. There's another day you might want to know about: Giving Tuesday. The idea is pretty straightforward. On the Tuesday after Thanksgiving, shoppers take a break from their gift-buying and donate what they can to charity.

Bill Gates

You're never going to get the amount of CO_2 emitted to go down unless you deal with the one magic metric, which is CO_2 per kilowatt-hour.

Bill Gates

Your most unhappy customers are your greatest source of learning.

Bill Gates

This page is intentionally left blank .

This page is intentionally left blank

This page is intentionally left blank

This page is intentionally left blank

This page is intentionally left blank

www.ingramcontent.com/pod-product-compliance
Lightning Source LLC
Chambersburg PA
CBHW071223280526
45787CB00002B/784